OUR LADY OF BEWILDERMENT

BARATARIA POETRY

Ava Leavell Haymon, Series Editor

OUR LADY OF
BEWILDERMENT

poems

ALISON PELEGRIN

Louisiana State University Press

Baton Rouge

Published by Louisiana State University Press
lsupress.org

LSU Press Paperback Original   .

Designer: Barbara Neely Bourgoyne
Typeface: Sina Nova

Cover image: *Electrons,* 2021, by Kristin Kwan

Library of Congress Cataloging-in-Publication Data
Name: Pelegrin, Alison, author.
Title: Our lady of bewilderment : poems / Alison Pelegrin.
Description: Baton Rouge : Louisiana State University Press, [2022] |
    Series: Barataria poetry
Identifiers: LCCN 2021022469 (print) | LCCN 2021022470 (ebook) | ISBN
    978-0-8071-7679-5 (paperback) | ISBN 978-0-8071-7717-4 (pdf) | ISBN
    978-0-8071-7718-1 (epub)
Subjects: LCGFT: Poetry.
Classification: LCC PS3566.E363 O97 2022 (print) | LCC PS3566.E363
    (ebook) | DDC 811/.54—dc23
LC record available at https://lccn.loc.gov/2021022469
LC ebook record available at https://lccn.loc.gov/2021022470

CONTENTS

I

RITUALS FOR SERVING AMBROSIA

DOOMSDAY'S DAUGHTER

I've been anxious since forever,
haunted by medieval premonitions
and my own. Forget Barbies and babysitting—
I was on the lookout for war planes
blacking out the sky. Faithful to calamity,
I assumed that every day might end
with a flash flood or category 5.
When lightning struck the telephone line
I felt it in my lips. When my teeth rattled
after a barge exploded on the Mississippi
I stashed my PJs in a bug-out bag.
I thought darkness might descend
on a day when the sky was a prism
of rain and shine, but my father said
it only meant the devil was beating
his wife. We went for ice cream
and I forgot about the questions I had
for death, that moment beyond breath
when the mind winds down to its halt.

ROYAL ANCESTRY

I ate sweet rolls and chickens pecked the door
while my people at the table carried on
in French, playing cards and peeling crabs.
We cursed in voodoo at football on tv,
and when Chester got sick we pushed him
everywhere, even on trips to the Gulf Coast casinos.
Aren't we all guilty of shooting for the fur-coat life,
with king crab for breakfast and comp nights
in casino hotels? If you squint you could say
we won—we were Carnival rich
with a chest of doubloons in jewel colors.
Uncle Royal called me queen and I believed
because he wore coattails spangled with sequins.
I rode his shoulders, and the Krewe
of Choctaw's feathered horses curtseyed.
Their riders tossed silk roses at our feet.
Grandmother's chin hairs frizzed in the dark
and the wet house sank into itself,
and across the Mississippi River, New Orleans
glittered, a string of pearls just out of reach.
I never belonged over there, but in Gretna
I was royalty—at the pawn shop, at the Camel Club
where my father ministered to shaky addicts
and drunks, his wailing infants of sobriety.
All of us royalty—former hard-drinking welders
and kings, fat on shrimp for as long as we could keep
the boat. St. Joseph's Day, and look at my son,
starring as Jesus Christ in the pageantry—
Mary and Joseph traveling door to door
seeking shelter and rest. For the finale,
an altar of food, and at the center
my royal boy cradled in the braided loaves.

BILDUNGSROMAN

Awake, asleep, I don't know what I was
in childhood, feeling things deeply
or not at all. It was a bad time for secrets.
Kudzu laid hands but failed to cleanse me
of the cruelties I exacted and received.
When I asked to ride a horse on my birthday,
I did not mean tracing circles on an invisible lead.
I wanted my steed mean-spirited
and wild, scattering clamshells up the levee
to race cargo ships and the rust-bottomed barges
shouldered above my head by the Mississippi.
How can it be so easy to force water
to change its shape? The mean girls next door
called through the fence, begging
for me to join them in the pool. As quick
as I could scuff down the driveway
I was there, fumbling with the locked gate
while they laughed. Likewise, I followed my brother
to the skate ramp, well aware a broomstick
was coming for the spokes of my bike.
I remember braiding a ribbon
in my ever-damp ponytail for the occasion
and afterward recording the long sad tale
in my diary, which I hid in plain sight.

Astrology, aquamarine, Tarpon Rodeo—what gave
birth to my silly belief that I was part fish?
Catfish probably—sleek and abundant, a bottom feeder
dragging whiskers through mud with a humorous and wise
expression. I took my birth sign Pisces literally,
felt twin fish tickle where my heart should be, checked for
gills and translucent patches of scales. The Magic 8-Ball
hinted, most often, *outlook not so good,* but only an
idiot would trust predictions floating in toilet bowl water.
Juggling my secret piscine ways was easy at first—mermaid
kicks dodging make-believe krakens and crocodiles in the pool,
legs twitching while sleep dragged me to an underwater
mermaid world. When mom lifted me, one day, from my
noon-hour nap, I was like a drowned thing,
obedient, but weepy and confused, dry-mouthed,
pulling sandals on my flipper feet. You'd never guess that I was
quasi-royalty, but my people were revered at the Tarpon
Rodeo all because of my uncles' boat, christened *The Stripper.*
Scanning the Gulf, we waiting hours for her to return,
trawl-speed, boasting a monster fish hoisted
upside down by gaff hook. I turned my back to her—
vessel unworthy of its catch-turned-burnished-figurehead, un-
worthy of the catcalls, as though reeling fish from ocean to
extinction was to be praised. Trophy fish stacked on ice
yawped into the evening, and I cried over the shine
zapped from their unzipped bodies, emptied and stacked by size.

EVEN IN GRETNA, HEARING THE CASHIER TALK, I LONG FOR GRETNA

after Basho

Coasting into my old world to help
mom pack up the house she can't sell
for nothing rimmed as it is with trash
and canals threatening to overflow
I get a taste for the red drink
of my youth and when the cashier
at the gas station lets slip the drawl
of my people most of them scattered
elsewhere or to the grave I could sob
peacock talk purposely showy and slow
any time I'd hit the twang mom got angry
because I was *letting my Gretna show*
she threatened a face slap or taste of soap
and I circled on a red bike just out of reach

OUR LADY ON THE HALF SHELL

Bathtub Madonna, lily of so many gardens,
    Queen of Heaven in the scalloped shell
of an oyster grand enough to hold you as its pearl,
    if only your goodness would take root.
You make two-lane highways worth traveling.
    Whitewashed, with marble chips or pansies
at your feet, you have many faces—blank alabaster,
    hand-painted Creole or coffee or midnight skin
with milky eyes peering out. You're motionless,
    a mannequin for grass skirts and Mardi Gras beads,
for waterline stains from time spent submerged
    in summer floods. They say no matter how
Katrina tore up house and yard, the half-shell Marys
    stayed put, never looking away from us in our distress.
We will always honor you with flower crowns,
    like our real mothers. When we sink your cement
likeness to keep fishermen from bombing rivers
    for an easy catch, it works. One look from you,
and they drop their dynamite in shame. Silent lady—
    arms at your sides as though you have nothing
to offer but the ground at your feet. Pray for us.

QUICKSILVER

Katrina, 2005

The horizon has always silvered
in the distance if I stare too long,
a molten rope, liquid air
lifting like flies over roadkill.
It happens on car trips, on long walks,
even scanning the asphalt
in search of my runaway dog.
Once, I hypnotized myself
on a swing, tricked by a quicksilver wrinkle.
I dozed off and fell, and when
I opened my mouth to scream,
playground debris grated in my teeth.

When the edges of the world turn watery
they are supposed to disappear.
I submit. That truth has sunken in:
quicksilver visions wrinkle,
and then they vanish. But
this water is absolute. It remains,
though the hurricane is over.
I have studied from my exile
in this hotel room, witnessed
rooftop rescue, the folly
of mammoth sandbags. This water
is no silvered mirage. It clings like tar.
It swallows everything we are.

BIOPIC

It was a relief to be told, in sixth grade,
that people knew I was a virgin by my walk.
There was no need to pretend anymore,
since my footsteps told all, or my face
flashing its which-fork-do-I-use vibe.
Look at me drunk, lost, turning to the moon
for answers, on a bridge dropping bread
to slime-backed turtles just in case a director
needs details for the movie of my life. It's a sad tale
of how sometimes I got sent to bed early,
while it was still light out. I don't know why.
But I had an afghan of neon granny squares
and V. C. Andrews books to read in secret.
I had another diversion, which was to isolate
one bump on the popcorn ceiling and try never
to lose sight of it. Sometimes I was the speck,
backtracking through space and time
to find my lamp-lit window.
I was the icon housed within, my braids
pulling apart as I peered through darkness
at the willow tree across the street. That summer
I highlighted every word in *The Witch
of Blackbird Pond* and fed the pages to a river
with a Choctaw name, thus completing the ritual.

SUCKER

I was a sucker for my daddy, an addict at heart,
always hooked on something—Drambuie,
the cabbage soup diet, Cajun dancing,
hauling Yankees on the tour bus up and down
River Road to ogle whitewashed plantations.
He once LARPed the vampire Lestat rising
from a grave because he was a sucker for Anne Rice.
He was a sucker for Wicks-n-Sticks, specifically
candles shaped like Buddha, and apartment living
after his divorces. He went hook, line,
and sinker for self-help, especially *Dianetics,*
and though his toenails blackened, he ran across
the longest bridge in the world. Twice.
Then he took up ballroom dancing. He was
the world's best drunk, and after he dried out
he was a sucker for AA. He was a sucker
for fathering offshoremen bailed from the drunk tank,
for naming these chain-smoking men my uncles,
the women my aunts. Life became a potluck
of talking through the night while the kids slept in cars.
Except for me. I was a sucker for sitting under the fig tree
behind the Camel Club thinking no one could see me
study him, golden-haired and calm, everyone's father
but mine. A sucker for calm, for burnt coffee and all-nighters,
for not looking away when sobriety's Adams
named the worst horrors of their lives.

UP AND DOWN THE RIVER

It began innocently, with field trips, ferries across the river
to emerald-green picnic spots, but my ruin began on the Mississippi's

resurrected battlegrounds. I straddled cannons at Confederate
Fort Jackson, that brick, five-pointed, fallen star of the Mississippi.

Its monuments of grass tell lies, as if peace could exist
while cannons radiate heat and aim at ghosts on the Mississippi.

The guards ride horses and convicts wear white for the rodeo
at Angola Prison, a plantation bound on three sides by the Mississippi.

I rode shotgun with my father, his tour bus making corkscrew turns
on River Road to showcase plantations on the Mississippi,

pure confection. I watched brides-to-be seduced by oak trees
and hoopskirt dreams of moonlit weddings on the Mississippi.

In the big house, our busload of guests ate cornbread and grits.
We split a packed lunch and skipped stones on the Mississippi.

His history books came to me, and I hear his voice narrating
the highlighted words, sins of omission on the Mississippi.

Our name is recorded in the book of confederate dead, making me
the worst thing, ruined and loyal, a daughter of rebels on the Mississippi.

DENIM AND DIAMONDS

Due to my preference for clover crowns
and cartwheeling in the grass,
I was an outfielder of all sports,
never once scoring or saving a game.
Who could blame me? Instead of soccer,
I would have prefered the pageant circuit.
To prepare, I smiled until my face
cramped, starved myself with dreams of a dress
so heavy with shine that I stumbled
everywhere, like a mermaid out of water.
As far as pageantry was concerned,
I never made it past dance recitals.
Most girls excelled at toe and tap,
but I was always in a pout, a back-row
waitress or gypsy upstaged by my uncles
with their intermission drag routine.
They practiced the moves all year, and
it was funny the first time—
cheerleaders with stuffed bras, my dad
center stage as gold lamé Marilyn Monroe.
I tried to stay mad, to turn away, but I watched
from the wings in velvet shadows,
my hand oscillating with an unanswered wave
to no one while they stole the show.

RITUALS FOR SERVING AMBROSIA

If not praying, if not bewitching slot machines,
my people are somewhere eating. They step outside
to swoon with the stars and their shadows spill
up the stoop, arms touching like paper dolls.
Sweet, earthly creatures. Ambrosia is theirs.
Nectar of the South, on no page of the low-carb bible.
A cherry-pinned froth of whipped cream, satsumas,
coconut flakes, pineapple tidbits, marshmallows,
pecans from Grandpa Hip's backyard. Confection
snubbed by snobs as a poor folks' food.
For me it's a birthday dish, a humble nectar
suitable for the card-table banquets of my kind—
angels with skin flap wings, with beards and tattoos,
with buck knives hidden under blankets in the truck.

FEAST OF THE CAJUN NAVY

My head's so crowded with giggles and snark
I'm called irreverent, mistaken for drunk
because I'm goofy after one Bloody Mary
on Mardi Gras, or at the roller derby
running of the bulls. Feast day every day.
I'm ready to take to the streets, parade
behind coffins or icons made of corn.
What can I feast today? How can I praise
the Cajun Navy, my patron saints, rescue boaters
cruising flooded streets, who sweet talk
the distressed from drowned cars and rooftops?
They came for me once, got me to the hospital
in time for a breathing treatment. I rest easy knowing
someone with a boat has my back. Hallelujah!

II

RAZOR DAYS

OUR LADY WHO THINKS SHE IS A SAINT

Sentimentality is something I detest,
little shrines everywhere
for acorns and umbilical cords,
but I started off the normal way,
believing my tea party guests—
koala, pony, duck—were real children.
Leaving them behind to go to school—
I thought that was suffering
and as penance I entered a Catholic phase,
saying no to everything and developing
warped beliefs about sainthood that involved
hairshirts, hunger, and sleep bereft of plush.
Poor sock monkey with the pompoms
chewed off—that was the one I kept,
working out a threadbare iconography
for the prayer card of my dreams.
Turns out I was rehearsing motherhood
before nursing offspring of my very own.
Poor lambs—I dressed them, offered
the breast milk of resentment for show.
Yes of course I woke them for meteor showers,
but also I sat them for long stretches, like dolls,
so that someone would need me forever.

THE PELEGRIN IN HER PIETY: A LINGO SONNET

Louisiana State Flag: Pelican in her piety; "Union, Justice, Confidence"
A lingo sonnet after Barbara Hamby

Medieval pelican with a trio in the nest, you tear your breast open
on Louisiana's flag, but your blood-milk piety is muted to a single drop.
Queen of bestiaries and stained glass, lone feathered martyr
spraying gore—by name alone we could be twins. We share the deepest
urge—motherhood's ogre love—a blur that comforts and devours, where shiv
wounds, pinches, and nips are stifled by sheer will. In my hand the ax
yields to a child's voice, quieting in my skull the flies that buzz.
Alpha-angel with a sword of fire, that's me the instant any cherub
cries. And you, pelican, of shore birds the wolf, you crash dive to feed,
elbow wings akimbo, throating so many fish you can't lift off.
Greed is one defense, but famine empties even the glutton's mouth.
Impossible horror crowds the world, and I fight fist and fang, and my mojo
kills. Even you, my doves, I could kiss you to death, squeeze you, kill, kill,
    kill.

FLOOD SUBJECT

I'm partial to the lesser saints
doers like my mom a mystic
of tropical storms making a game
of disaster making it safe for us to nap
in hammocks under the carport a marvel
of calm and when her crisis strength
kicked in able to lift the living room set
up on cinder blocks how many times
have I waded in floodwaters sheened with oil
or put my faith in sandbags and the altar
she erected in haste on the coffee table
flashlights a radio a deck of cards
hurricane candles housing gaudy saints
other than illumination no real power

BRAIN FEVER

In the goody-goody books of my youth, girls swooned
when the mysteries of weakness and will
overwhelmed. They fainted, collapsed in a fog
that drew the family for a bedside vigil, waking
from a riotous sleep to find all problems solved.
You handled things differently, with a baseball bat,
chasing bike thieves to make them apologize.
Do you remember locking the front door,
forcing me to fight? When I turned to face
my bully, I kicked his meat so hard that I felt bone.
I never wanted to be tough. I know it's the pills,
but I hate the new you—my unwanted child—endlessly
puzzled, a chart for everything, including a black mark
when you think the upstairs neighbor kicks his dog.
We used to joke about the men in white coats,
but I see how this will end. You're a stranger mom.
In the ER (twice this week) you tell about the voices
and the plots I'm scheming against you.
Handle your business. Bang a broom on the ceiling,
trigger the fire alarm late at night, because you need to drop
the marionette routine and go back to how you were—
unhinged but in command, kind hearted, kind of mean,
mastermind of punishments that outstripped the crimes.

OUR LADY OF THOUGHTS AND PRAYERS

I'm the weary saint of those who sorrow least,
wind in white flags whistling from a better place,
puddle-skinned, one of the drowned, part beast.
I'm your hothouse hope, your gasps, your crawl space
after the levees break and while the shooter aims.

My cult distributes cardboard meals.
My cult links arms, lights votives in the street,
they sob ten-deep in school yard vigils
clutching at love and light, their idols.
I'm the banshee conjured by the battered world.

I'm the banshee conjured by the battered world
clutching at love and light, their idols
while they sob ten-deep in school yard vigils.
My cult links arms, lights votives in the street,
My cult distributes cardboard meals.

After the levees break and while the shooter aims,
I'm your hothouse hope, your gasps, your crawl space.
I'm puddle-skinned, one of the drowned, part beast.
I'm wind in white flags whistling from a better place,
the weary saint of those who sorrow least.

DOLLY

If I could occupy myself once more
with the industry of youth—
tearing posters of heartthrobs
out of magazines while the record player
heard my confessions—
I'd go back to believing
my mother might morph into Dolly Parton.
Or at least someone less frumpy
who would let me wear lip gloss.
It was my one wish. My only prayer.
Forget logistics, I assumed
her transformation would happen overnight
and rub off on me. I assumed that one day
she would wake in full makeup
and a halter top, and sing my name.
Before I started coming home wasted,
before she dragged me inside by my hair,
there was hope for us.
We didn't hate each other. I just wanted
a change, did everything I could
to prepare the way.

WALK-THROUGH

No, she won't take a picture of me
and my brother in front of the door
etched with decades of our growth.
Instead she re-dusts corners on hand
and knee because she fears the neighbor
who bought this storm-patched house
plans to roll in with her book club to gawk.
We are as tall as we will ever be,
and this is what it's like to be owned.
Mom is stooped and skittish like my aunt,
a housekeeper who cut hair on the side.
She embarrassed me, but I smoked the same
menthols as she did, stashing them in the grill
on the patio, where I had a front row seat
to wildness in the dream house next door.
Those kids backslid in the ways of the rich,
raiding a pantry the size of my bedroom,
shoplifting tennis whites, flipping cars
on the golf course. I never saw them defend
against a hair brush or slotted spoon.
Their beatings looked like pats on the back.
They slept late, I rode my bike to three jobs
and perfected the art of keeping score.
Decades later, I'm only half-faking my hard-on
for revenge against these razzle-dazzle
pampered bitches snapping their fingers
to get my mom's attention.

OUR LADY OF THE FLOOD

Louisiana, August 2016

Lady, is that you, with a citronella halo,
ghosting the mud-milk waters
with a laundry basket of kittens in one arm?
You are no mythic Saint Medard, sheltered
from rain beneath an eagle's wing,
but a hands-on angel of the earthly kind—
sweaty, with a burden of buckets and bleach,
surefooted through labyrinths of debris.
You take meals in church parking lots,
thankful for whatever is served.
Some saints are untouchable behind glass,
but you ride in open boats
with mildew on the edges of your gown,
a calm commander of the Cajun Navy's fleet.
Your devotees worship outside
in a circle of ruined pews,
no incense but bug spray, their voices
a capella because the music of the drowned piano
is too sad to sing to. They remain faithful
because you are the one constant,
honored in front gardens and kitchen shrines.
You with your shrimp boots and rubber gloves—
without flinching you lead and they follow,
walking on water in the safety of each other.

RAZOR DAYS

Blood. That's what we inherited. Blood,
crumpled white petals of gauze, powdered gloves
stripped inside out. We kicked in the door,
and light blared around us like a ladder of knives,
overexposing dust motes, the box cutter,
and other wreckage of her deeds. A wonder
we didn't see it coming. She left clues everywhere—
nonsense notes, curio shelves purged
of our childish handmade offerings. Clinical,
efficient, we made quick work of the cleanup,
peeling away the mattress pad, cramming ruined
pillows into contractor bags. No arguments, no tears,
and not a shred of evidence. She'd have been proud of us
thieving in broad daylight, ditching proof in the trash.

I called 911. On the line, I was icy to Dispatch
and then relieved when the hospital took over.
I cowered away from her, across the room.
They closed her up, tossed her bloody socks,
and eventually I ushered my wordless brother
bedside, not because he insisted, but because
I couldn't do it anymore. We've never agreed
on anything, but since this we talk every night.
When we hang up I can slash a line through the day.
We were mean at first. We wanted her punished,
and then we rushed to bring her slippers and a robe
in lockdown. We waited with empty pockets in the room
with no clocks, just a white board with the menu
and the date, the wrong date, Suicide Eve, in red.

I'm in no mood for rejoicing, but I acknowledge
the comfort of routine, even the habits of a few weeks.
Since a prayer should begin with praise, I'll do my best
to remember locking my phone away, signing the book,
waiting to be buzzed in. On time or not, the minutes
count against our glass-walled hour. With nothing
to say, I welcome interruptions of sound and smell,
the diversion of Mr. _____ who announces his strip-tease
by triggering the fire alarm. I never feared him.
Each day like a crow I made my offering—a cactus
confiscated by the one she called Nurse Ratched,
forbidden stick of Doublemint tucked in *Reader's Digest*.
A rulebreaker to the bone, she palmed the gum, and this
conspiracy let me believe she was in there somewhere.

To be fair, I should mention the good times, free rein
on our bikes, the easy-to-remember rule of summer:
dish soap lather on the Slip-n-Slide counts as a bath.
We muddied ourselves wading in filthy canals
and instead of fussing she laughed at our ruined clothes.
She understood the uncool neon of new shoes
and would back over my Tretorns with the car
until they were acceptably scuffed. By any measure
she loved us well. Even with the risk of manhole covers
bubbling up and unleashing a suction that could
siphon a child beneath the street, she let us roam
barefoot in floodwaters. We emerged unharmed,
blissfully unaware of the dangers, wasting our shrieks
on minnows who in confusion nibbled at our feet.

She's always been the same, confrontational
with the truth, telling it like it is in too much detail
for family or strangers like when my kid brother
flipped the bird and she pounced, grabbed his hand,
saying *this is the dick, these are the balls, and it means*
fuck you! How proud she was to display blood clots
I'd soon endure, chicken gizzards in the toilet bowl.
And now she's an exhibitionist with these puffed scars—
she gives a play-by-play, and for an encore lifts
the circle scarf twined around her neck. A terror to me,
the cleanup. I can't stop thinking of that campfire story
about the girl with the yellow ribbon who somehow
survived high school, but one tug at that choker
and she's a Gorgon, her lips still moving, and her hair.

Liquor cabinets, soft-core porn—I was virginal
in every dimension before sleepovers, as clueless
about Spanish fly as about life in other families,
the takeaway being that in my house everything
was wrong. Mom worked late, and at home
blocked me from the kitchen while scooping ice cream
for my brother. I would never have been allowed
to order pizza, to watch—with friends!—from the bed
while she sipped wine and slipped in and out
of sequined gowns. In other houses this was routine,
the surplus of snacks and party clothes, relaxed attitude
I tried so hard to adopt. Who cares *who shot J. R.?*
I was always last to strip and squat over the hand mirror,
mortified by the rawness crammed inside of me.

It's a miracle when my gentleness returns.
The leaves are emerald-glossed, swiping at the sky.
Why do I rejoice? The mom-child lives,
and she charms me with her easy delights—
Valentine scarf, Mardi Gras wreath on her door,
how she walks a short path and asks about the birds.
Chickadees cling to the feeder outside her window,
and my avian heart hammers when she says their name.
Worries await if I look off the page of the day,
so I choose instead to eat the candies she set out
in a crystal dish. She wants to feed me, to stuff
my pockets with small gifts, and I accept.
We laugh remembering boiled eggs in a meatloaf
on my birthday years ago. She called it meatloaf surprise.

FEAST OF MY MEDJUGORJE LIES

Dear ones, perfect strangers, I confess
I'm guilty of Medjugorje lies. I never
climbed a mountain on my knees
for a glimpse of her, but said I did.
Everyone yapped about miracles,
pointed to nothing and called it her face,
a heart-shaped shadow in white
shading the crowns of trees.
While pretending not to look, I checked
everywhere for my angel—the night sky,
the faces of statues on the verge of tears—
but caught no sign, was never healed.
I still seek her, she who wears a halo
made of weeds, who loves so much that it hurts.

III

RAGE GODDESS

OUR LADY OF WHATEVER

I shall require a toolbox shrine, with mirrored walls,
stuffed with party mints and candles stoked against
my legendary wrath, a target practice ace of spades
with all four corners clipped, and an alias worth
embroidering on pillows, inking on knucklebones.
But I'm a late-blooming lady, and the best names
have been dealt—Our Lady of Iguanas, her reptile crown,
Our Lady of Prompt Succor, New Orleans' queen,
whose magic halts floodwaters at the chapel steps.
Our Lady of Blind River, ghosting by pirogue
to her cypress abode. Our Lady of Sorrows,
heart worn outside her body, her only joy in life
to weep. So many lakes. So many Ladies of the Lakes.
Maybe I could be Lake Pontchartrain's Lady
of the Longest Bridge, Lady of Cicada Tea Parties,
of How Things Used to Be, or Sand Mandalas
Reduced to Cerulean Ash. Our Lady of Shrinky Dinks.
Our Lady of Darkness who skips eclipses, Our Lady
of Crash Diets and Devoted Avoidance of the Occult,
Our Lady of the Hot Flash, of Fractals behind the Eyes,
Día de los Deadlifts Lady, strong as a man.
Our Lady of Notebook Libations, the last few pages left blank.
Our Lady of Mystics, who arrives without knowing why,
who drifts, sometimes, with numbness and no purpose,
her intent awakened only when she lays down to rest.

MY SNATCH IS PRETTY GOOD

If you hear *pussy* when I say *snatch,* either
you belong to my cabal of weightlifting poet yogis,
or you're my mother, snatch the frequent star
of her dirty jokes. As explanation all I have
is that her father was a Marine with a vodka IV
who told home health to blow it out of their asses.
Hip!—we called him Hip—when I think of him,
I think of suicide—I saw how his eyes roved for that pistol,
and in my fear imagined a froth of blood pinking his undershirt
the exact color of the tank top I now wear to the gym,
which claims, in girly script, *My Snatch Is Pretty Good.*
An understatement, and a double entendre if you know
that in addition to vajayjay, *snatch* also refers
to that Olympic lift in which the barbell, with one pull,
travels from the ground to overhead. Because I'm giddy
with the miracle of speed and kilo math,
and my bouncing plates are so loud that other lifters
look my way—that's why I giggle when I hit a snatch.
But also because of my mom, who reminds me, even now,
when I screw up, to check myself because I used to live
"in her snatch." Considering our history,
I knew she would laugh at my tank top
and the bumper sticker version I bought for her
because I'm proud of all my women,
bad ass, indelicate broads, and me the same,
in a full squat bearing down with 60 kilos overhead,
the sweet spot where I find my balance.
I have felt a midwife's intimacy with other lifters,
our tribe gathered around the platform
as though awaiting a birth, only it's the barbell
we are waiting on, waiting for it to move,
willing with our minds, helping with yells if one
among us is buried under a squat, grinding to stand.

But it is the lifter who does all of the work,
as in birth it is the mother, alone and watched,
all eyes on her, on her snatch, vortex from which
daughters and sons emerge and unfold,
each of them a bloodied lotus, and the mother—
well, when it was me, I was stunned, amazed,
as with a personal best on the barbell. *What the hell
just happened? How did I do this?
Is there no end to my strength?*

HEIFER

No debutante, no sweet sixteen, in prom pics
freaky tall, exiled by the cheerleaders
from their pyramid but on-call as anchor
in a tug-of-war, bone crusher, hurler of javelins
at Sister Ambrose across the field. In yoga,
where we are all one, I am more like one and a half,
a starved-down XXL unable to swap clothes
with anyone I know. Frumpy, hugely maternal,
an elephant streaming tears as I move logs,
except I've grown to love the work of slinging weight.
Now, at the gym, having learned to strut my size,
I will settle on a bro to nitpick and outlift,
kilo plates rattling on the bar as I uproot it in a flash.
In high school, the nuns taught us that our thumbs
could poke out perverts' eyes. Protecting
our maidenhood, they made it seem like a sport,
and I couldn't wait to make the team, virginal
in the extreme, violently devoted and pure,
like the fantasy girl they praised, who dropped
to all fours, chewed grass, and mooed,
shitting her pants to stave off dishonor.
I got my chance to lash out against a man,
the cop who confiscated my fake ID
and drove me home, one hand on the wheel
and one under my shirt. I thought it was punishment
for my lies and amaretto buzz, so I held still,
and didn't claw his eyes out or bellow or screech.
He said I was lucky to get off with a warning,
and, recalling virgin martyr Saint Maria Goretti
and her 14 stab wounds, I suppose he was right.

EXCISING A MEMORIAL TO THE CONFEDERATE GENERAL ROBERT E. LEE

Lee Circle
New Orleans, LA
May 19, 2017

Confederate cake-topper, arms crossed
as if to shrug the bird shit off his shoulders—

of course he's got to go. So why the scrap
of rebel in me clinging to this piss-soaked ground

where his pillar stands, Mardi Gras memory lane, where
I puked through my nose, observed rats untie shoes

and tunnel up some guy's pants empty where the leg
should be? I never paid attention to Lee himself,

big man above, nicknamed King of Spades for ordering
soldiers just to dig in. And boy, he is rooted here, deep,

a ghost with disciples still, his Dixie gospel a fog
I breathe, complicit, sharing air with good ole boys

who glorify the past with choreographed reenactments
at Chalmette Battlefield, still pining for what would be

if the South had won. Same ones who genuflect
before bloodstained artifacts at the Confederate Museum

down the street. Field trips there left me convinced
I was superior, proud pariah of the antebellum world.

As one outsized, she-ogre huskier than any Yank
or Reb, I was partly right. But also I am Louisiana born,

with a rebel attitude entrenched, dug in, a belle genetically
unable to stand down, even though the Confederate general

Robert E. Lee commanded. I am his unwitting subject,
ready to lock horns over anything, including

the right to gawk at illustrations in a doctor's manual
held open to the page of hacksaws and hooks.

I read that they would tie men down, with the limb
to be excised dangling from the cot, knock them out

with opium or fists before applying the violence
needed, sometimes, to save a life. And so I cast myself

as killer angel in this tale, my gown a mop for blood,
my handiwork a regiment of empty sleeves

shaking their defiant, phantom fists at the sky.

RESTING BITCH FACE

The horror of finding myself documented
unawares in a photograph taken while I cheered
at my son's wrestling meet produced a shock
for which I was unprepared. My girth
was unfairly measured by the lens,

and though I have, in recovery from an injury
sustained while lifting weights competitively,
gained both softness and kilos, such changes
are not pronounced to the degree that the image
leads the onlooker to believe. Additionally revealed

is my double chin, emphasized by a covert attempt
to check my phone. *Slight* gut, *momentary* double chin—
these imperfections are easily explained.
But the phenomenon of my resting bitch face—
that prime unflattery—frankly, I wish Archimedes

or some other genius of classical antiquity
would chime in to solve for this scowl, worn here
in a moment of what I recall as mirth. A scowl
so exquisite that my son, pausing between victories,
notes that it is meme-worthy, and while his comment

was meant in jest, my face contorts, now sporting
the grimace of one who tasted a spider
when expecting honey on the tongue, or who realized
that his wave to the stands was intended not for me,
but for a girlfriend who possesses the thinness

and personality of a paper doll. The epiphany strikes
like a hen peck from behind. Am I bitchy?

Or even worse, bitter? True, my jokes are mean,
        and I talk shit, and left unguarded my lips smash
                into a frown. But I'm powerless over this tendency

            to ponder myself into a grumpy swoon
        while my kaleidoscopic mind bounces from thought
to thought. With shame, I dredge up the memory
        that I wore this face in my first picture
                with you, my son, when you were just born.

            I was exhausted, and I had blood in my hair,
        and all I could think was that I would die if you ever
pierced your ears. Now you can do whatever
        you want, because to me, you seem like a god.
                And I pause here to tip my honeyed wine

            to Sappho, her lost words ever on my mind. Sappho,
        another straight-mouthed beauty, her poetry
so revered her face was stamped on coins.
        The Greeks idealized the restraint of her
                archaic smile, but I see impatience written there,

            as though she knew her value would be diminished
        by the touch of many thumbs. In her face I see
myself, lips hiding a snarl, corners of the mouth curled
        to stifle what I *could* unleash, delicious, divine
                execrations on stand-by courtesy of the muse of mean.

OUR LADY OF "NO RAGRETS"

poem beginning with a misspelled tattoo

Our Lady of "No Ragrets," prevention of bad tattoos
must be your side hustle, a part-time ministry.
With respect, Queen of Inky Heaven,

a few too many permanent atrocities
have escaped your intervention. Just when it seems
the world of ink has collected its wits,

another troll with armpit hair is born,
or a Patrick Swayze centaur in a rainbow breeze.
So many RIPs, so many mama's boys. So many

portraits of you take liberties—from reverent
to sexy-but-still-chaste, to Día de los Muertos Mary—
rainbow kewpie with a fleshed-out skull, gown

lifted up revealing pistols on juicy, half-spread thighs.
Are you angry to have been made slutty
sweet lady? What's better—to be forgotten

or to mingle, on the flash-art wall, among vixens
with spade-tipped tails? Mother to so many
bad-inked guys and dolls, how do you stay calm?

My mother wept over my tattoo, a fish
in multicolor flames swimming up my back.
Bad ink claims *Nothing last's forever,*

except, of course, YOLO spelled in penises,
a jigsaw-puzzle face, and SORRY MOM
stamped across the knuckles of two fists.

But what about a mother's grief over children
delivered with no guarantees? They are born,
they whine, they steal change from your purse,

they pierce their ears and brand themselves with ice.
No blank space on their baby skin, to mark with kisses.
Only scribbles. Other people's names inside of hearts.

OUR LADY OF THE INGRATES

after Barbara Hamby

In-your-face irony has turned me into my mom—lame DJ,
killer of beer pong brackets, sleepless on the chaperone's vigil.
Mommy Dearest, I muttered while she sewed me in my prom gown,
offending even further with rolling eyes. I deserved the slap—
quasi-painful, but not as much as I let on. Ichor
sass spewed from me. Not even Tabasco could stop it,
unabashed pettiness snowballing from the cradle to the grave.
Wrathful saint of the long game, she stockpiled, in her Pandora's box,
younglings. From the payback soup primordial my boys emerged, blitz
avenging her with their shenanigans. It's karma's proverb,
catharsis for her as they toe the waters of the hell I raised,
emo/B.O./cock of the walk seesaw for me, with no hope for relief—
gimme-gimme ingrates, heartbreakers, tearing at me with relish.

RAGE GODDESS

after The Iliad

Rage, goddess, sing the rage of Irvin's daughter—
wasted, naked, raped. I fume, swoon, gag on the bile
of it, Achilles-like with my wild boar rage. I tried
meditating, but my mind is already empty—
all thoughts expunged except fury leading the way.
In Rage 101, my father was my guide, swatting
at stand-still objects with the weedwacker,
prowling around the car where I hid from him.
He was so crazed the neighbors called the cops.
I, too, have frightened my children, have ruined
snow days by yanking sonofabitching Christmas lights
from the attic. They were terrorized when I went
after the dog with a shovel because it snapped at them.
They stiffened when I swooped in for a kiss. Yoga
should have made me nicer, but all that's changed
is that my mean thinking happens upside down—
scenarios where the throat punch is permitted,
and knees to the face. In a stifling room, flanked
by skinny bitches, I shudder recalling the weight
on top of me, a bear of a man, a preppy beast, and who
would be stupid enough to take the drink from his hand?
That was the last time I didn't know my strength.
Now I keep a beating stick nearby, with splinters
on one end for extra hurt. Rage haunts me
with its vice grip on my heart, follows me
in sleep, where in the roller derby dream
they call me Bonecrusher. I'm ashamed
of my fantasies. I want to toss his soft parts
to the dogs. He'll writhe, and I'll tip my wine
to the flames—unrecognizable, blood-
spattered, with ashes smeared across my face.

APOLOGY

Why did I pretend to hate bunking
at Rosaryville for band camp?
My fixation on white-washed Jesus
in the sisters' cemetery was uncool—
I pretended to choose that path so I could sneak
cigarettes and conjure my pranks in peace.
My grandfather taught me to rub a bar
of soap over my double-socked toes—
thanks to that hack I could march forever
in my majorette boots. He also trained me
in Marine Corps hijinxs. It was my pleasure
to muffle a trumpet solo, to hop out of step
on purpose and keep it up for miles
just to see the sisters scowl. I loved Mardi Gras—
the parades, mammoth breasts painted with faces,
the crowd adorning my me and my horn
with beads that looked like fun-loving rosaries.
When I made up things to tell the priest
they sent in to hear confessions, more than the lies,
my intent was to make him feel useful.
I was clueless then, and only a few years removed
from having tangible regrets, like that night
in a honkytonk when I struck a match
on my zipper to keep a creep at bay. I knew
my plan backfired when he leaned in and whispered
hot pants. These days, drink in hand,
I boogie when the marching bands pass.
I don't know exactly what I'm sorry for,
but it's bothered me my whole life.

FEAST OF BANANA SPIDERS, STARLIGHT, AND ROADKILL

Amazing universe, all dance and dazzle—
sometimes it gets on my nerves.
The simplest things overwhelm—
the hummingbird's polite sipping of the iris,
banana spiders, their webs strung from power lines
like flat sheets hung to dry for the marathon
of my commute. Of course I yawp about it.
I woke up hoping for ordinary, looking for a fight,
but I tangled with mystery instead.
I can't see straight, can't keep track of it all.
Starlight slants through me and I'm shocked—
a deer caught in dwindling dawn. I'd make
a fantastic carrion bird—clueless,
cocky, every roadkill meal a banquet.

IV

THAT WHICH
DOES NOT KILL US

MESSENGER

after Diane Suess's American Sentence sonnets

Forcefield, invisible skin, the unseen fist that shoved me down the stairs
before the gunshots started—tell me, was it God, or luck, or am I
nuts? Was it you who dropped a bird to rest on the brim of my sunhat?
Whispered affirmation delivered with spite from a nun's fuzzed lip and
received by me with a snarl—was it chance, Messenger, or you? Stranger,
murky angel fluent in the speech of madmen and the pure of heart,
how could you know I learn best by apparition? I've had to fend for
myself during perilous, long silences, but you helped to reduce
my nagging worries with dreams—a do-over of my son's birth by way
of blade so that I felt my own strength as I gasped him into the world,
or my heart in a vice as another nightmare of death blasts through me—
blood-clot sky off the porch while the prismatic gears of creation tick-
tock to pitch black. Thanks, I guess—was that a spirit wind, forgetfulness
you sent?—for the distraction from my mind beating on and on, alone.

WALKING ON WATER

Bernhard Plockhorst, The Guardian Angel, *1886*

Guardian angels were hard for me to get behind
thanks to that infamous stormscape pastoral—
a hands-off charmer ready for her close-up
while rains and the night sky hound two children
across a snaggle-tooth bridge. The boy and girl
in tattered clothes—that was me and my brother,
and this portrait, shellacked on a rustic clock face,
shared wall space with our parents' zodiac signs
pyrographed in wood. Despite the odd logistics
of their union, I never questioned scorpion or goat.
But the guardian angel rubbed me wrong.
Doll-faced, detached, she seemed more worried
about her hair than the danger underfoot.
I knelt before the altar of bad art. I tried to believe,
but I knew that no matter how daintily
she fluttered, we would stumble, step on nails,
that the deluge would push inside and leave us
to begin again—again. Catechism failed me,
but not astrology. Scorpio and Capricorn
were of more crisis use than a diva hovering
out of danger's reach. I might have surrendered
if she terrified me, if some hint of hard times
shadowed her translucent face. But even then
I knew there was no praying away wind and rain.
The waters rise or they don't, it's nothing personal.

MYTH OF MYSELF

Coonass mystic is an easy sell, an explanation
    for the regional, ancestral bitterness

I pass off as a mystery. Also I have fancied myself
    a jester of the bayou, sage among dimwits,

passing a good time and writing poems
    in my shame-tamed ragin' Cajun accent.

My name embroidered on a bookmark—
    Alison—means "truthful one" in Greek,

a stretch, though I ran with it.
    I made no claim to be part wolf after the dog

tore open my face, but never denied it either,
    polishing that story like a gem—rancid fear,

gash in my cheek so wide I saw my teeth
    snarling down from the ER's mirrored lights.

I'm a Pisces and I know I'll never drown.
    I give off a riot-ready vibe. No one

comes close enough to notice my childish hobbies—
    cross stitching profanities, collecting

miniature bone china creatures, believing in magic
    because bashful ferns shutter at my touch.

MYSTERIA

I cringe to recall the blue morpho's pop
at the Zen garden where mistakenly I stomped
a butterfly and golden koi kept vigil
with the speckled flames of their bodies
every summer night squandered
not one bottle of wine shared with the moon
I am no Buddhist the fading world
is all about me—one question
splendid beloved what's the true name
for those white blooms you called *mysteria*
and another how can I still be learning
to title life's marvels emerald pulse
of a hummingbird cupped in one hand
the tidal wind that pulls through tiny flowers

REGARDING MY PROLONGED ABSENCE FROM CHURCH

My leavetaking began with an Irish goodbye
that felt like a journey to the underworld.
The gimmicky sermons made me groan,
and I had one foot out the door ever since
they voted to allow a horror movie
to film inside—altar, loft, pews stuffed
with monsters. So what if the money
went to organ repairs. Just like Christmas,
Easter—I couldn't unsee the vicious faces.
When some Buddhists came to town
and taught my sons to paint with sand,
I loved that they never turned to see
who followed as they walked to the river.
Not one word was spoken. When I left
small change for a waitress at the bottom
of a water glass, I blamed the devils
of sixth grade, but it was me revealing the poverty
of my own soul. Try explaining that to the choir,
or singing with such a stone in your mouth.
It was much easier to recognize the pauses
between cypress trees as holy ground, and walk away.

OUR LADIES OF THE QUARANTINE

As we plod through quarantine, one plus is dudes
not prescribing smiles beneath our masks. We can relax,
take deep breaths in down dog before breakfast
to shake loose the terror of the red-sky dreams.

Relaxed, smiling or not beneath our masks, we dream
of solitude, of sitting in the laundromat watching the dryers spin,
of waking, for once, untouched by the terror of the red-sky dream.
Two months in, we yearn for the old monotony, the old routine—

Om at the laundromat while the dryers spin.
What's our fantasy if we are the last ones left?
Something reckless or getting back to the herbalist routine?
Maybe shed the yoga pants for something military, green?

There's a lot of freedom for the last ones left.
We could make a special trip for box wine and chocolate.
We could go yogis-turned-survivalists, dressed in green,
camouflaged from bare-faced bandits creeping around.

Now it feels sinful to shop for box wine and chocolate,
to take comfort in TP rolls stashed in the closet.
The bare-faced bandits spread conspiracies around.
When the numbers climb, they say it's no big deal.

When TP dwindles and things just don't seem right,
our drinking starts at noon. Things are so far gone.
The numbers spike, the graph looks like a cliff
and we squandered days on pedicures and yoga.

Day drinking helps blur the brain, but there's no escaping
portable morgues, birds rising like ashes in the sky.

We wasted good lives on paintball and yoga,
ignored sunsets no matter how pink the fire.

Dumpster fire days. No shy smiles under the masks,
no looking away from portable morgues, cinder birds in the sky.
There's no telling a sunset from the world on fire. We give in,
breathe deeply in down dog at the beginning of the end.

DELUGE: A TRIPLE SONNET

after Dorothy Chan

Bless my grumbling soul! This poem came
        in the shower and so begins with a jolt of steam
at the tail end of January in the year of the rat,
        and it comes to me I ought to praise rising waters
for making possible my exposure to fondue,
        voted best comfort food in a blackout, and who
doesn't like cocktail weenies dipped in cheese?
        It comes to me that I can move things
with my mind—hereditary, I believe, because I trust
        mother, despite her flaws, would have managed to lift
any railcar I happened to be wedged beneath.
        I have never saved a life, but I have snatched a barbell
overhead—repeatedly—with no clear idea of how—
        and that, friends, is the topic of an essay I plan to write:

Weight Lifting and Poetry: Sister Arts of Physics,
        Mind Fog, and Stubborn Will. My mini Coke Zero fizzles,
a distraction. Side-eyed through the window I see my neighbor
        needs his grass cut. He pays in deer sausage
for me to keep watch during his weekends at the hunting camp.
        Surely he knows I would do it for nothing.
I gather his paper and mail, and sometimes a haiku happens:
                On the gravel driveway
            snails trace filigree labyrinths
                on yesterday's news.
Judging from his tattoos, today's yoga teacher
        was in special ops, and I know I would die
in a war zone flapping my peacekeeper mouth,
        no grip strength anymore to heave myself

one-handed into the helicopter hovering impatiently.
   I'm off barbells now except as spotter for my son
benching big numbers. None of the other mothers
      can do that. This year as I herald spring I have decided
it is purple flowers I will invite to die in the drought
      of my garden—safe haven exclusively to armadillos
and mint. Every year on my birthday I wish for
      one of those backyard barrels that captures rainwater,
even though an owl could drown, and leave me
      handfishing for a feathered football. How do they fly
with a gut full of stones? How do we live, knowing as we do
      that days run off wasted, water down the drain?
Keats's tombstone overwhelms us with the truth—
      Here lies One Whose Name was writ in Water.

THE CLOSE PART

I called it *The Close Part,* my invisible way
of knowing, a familiar without face
or voice. The Close Part came and went,
some nights storming with time's blood troops
through my mind, and others climbing
gingham's frills to get to my throat.
I would have preferred to braid the hair
of off-limits Madame Alexander dolls,
but it watched while I pretended to sleep.
Adults kept their distance, like they knew
I was an old soul, one who could sense
lightning before it struck but not
bird shit in my ponytail. The Close Part
called and I answered. I don't know why.
One time I knelt before an electric socket,
leaned in until my eyeball touched and was zapped.
A wet bandana blindfold cooled my eyes.
In traffic on the Mississippi River bridge,
I considered jumping, though I knew
what would happen—every bone broken,
regret the long way down. Head out the window,
hand on the door, the concrete a blur
as the car inched along—I came *this* close.

OUR LADY OF BEWILDERMENT

When I turn fifty, instead of a boudoir shoot
I'm having prayer cards made that feature me
as my alter ego, *Our Lady of Bewilderment.*
I'll be in yoga pants, reclining mid-swoon on the couch
completely overwhelmed as I so often am
by the state of wonder buzzing in my brain.
I have time to settle on my iconography
provided I do not die of my distractions—
the pebbles push-pinned in my bare feet
as I speed-walk down hot asphalt straining my eyes,
unable to see the comet for the trees. Verso
will be words, a blessing I have yet to write.
I would like to write a poem about the button
in my driveway, most certainly a gift from crows.
I would like to formalize my blacktop beatitudes
with a wine glass in one hand, and a Le Pen in the other.
A little bit cloister, a little bit drama queen,
I'm caught between worlds, a glutton for wonder
begging for more. Nothing over the top,
because I'm not searching for affliction,
and I don't have a mystic's patience or time,
just a little bit of oooh and ahhh to jumpstart
days which otherwise are uniform—
culvert steam, hornets, asphalt, a diesel wind.

SOLILOQUY AGAINST A KUDZU BACKDROP

Audience of none, superstition dictates
that I peek through the kudzu curtain
like a starlet before making an entrance
and speaking yet again on the theme
of ignorance observed in waking life.
I would like to believe these are extras
in a movie, good ole boys play acting,
rather than my neighbors, some of them
so far gone that I can't decide if I should
relocate or wait for the punchline.
I slip up sometimes, thinking we are friends,

but they're dangerous. Too many guns,
and "heritage, not hate" is still a thing.
Today they laughed, like I knew they would,
when I delighted as a swallow-tail kite
dove for nestlings. How can we be
so different when the the same trees
rustle in all of our dreams? Something wild
stirs in me. Something wild calls my name,
and vanishes, muffled beneath a beast
of green. When I look up nothing's left
but the ghost of wind lurching through kudzu leaves,
the movement of a horse minus the horse itself.

THAT WHICH DOES NOT KILL US

I have prayed in all the different ways,
oversharing my ecstasy and shame.
I used my third eye as a bullshit detector,
and in response the azaleas bloomed
with gusto. I rode the mechanical bull
like I always wanted. I had my hand tattooed,
not for luck, but as a reminder that all I want
is to finish a good poem and let it go
on a river that flows away from me.
At the grocery store the windows rattle,
but it isn't raining yet. I've got time
to sample pork cracklings and moonshine,
to raise my thimble cup. We think we are angels
attempting to calm this sparrow trapped
in the produce section. Poor creature—it's terrified.
By accident, or miracle, we usher it outside.

FEAST WITH A MOUTHFUL OF BEES

I was doomsday's daughter, ignoring the hum
of everyday ungilded twitching things.
Ecstatic, enraged, brimming with questions
and lies, I stumbled through violent
and ordinary times with a drink in each hand,
my head crowded with cusses and snark
and the sound of me screaming underwater.
Razor days—I'd rather cough up fishhooks
than try to understand. Long list of harms
with wonders mixed in—can it be enough?
The words sting—bees on my tongue.
I vibrate from the inside out. I call on strangers
to testify that sometimes I weep for no reason,
that clover fills my footsteps as foretold.

ACKNOWLEDGMENTS

Grateful acknowledgment to the publications where the following poems first appeared:

Bennington Review: "Our Lady of Thoughts and Prayers," "Doomsday's Daughter," and "Feast with a Mouthful of Bees"; *Broadsided:* "Quicksilver" and "Feast of Banana Spiders, Starlight, and Roadkill;" *Cherry Tree:* "Our Lady of 'No Ragrets'" and "Our Lady of Whatever"; *The Cincinnati Review:* "Our Lady on the Half Shell"; *Crazyhorse:* "Flood Subject" and "Our Lady of Bewilderment"; *Diode:* "Rituals for Serving Ambrosia" and "Soliloquy against a Kudzu Backdrop"; *Electric Lit:* "Bildungsroman" and "Regarding My Prolonged Absence from Church"; *Gettysburg Review:* "That Which Does Not Kill Us"; *Gulf Coast:* "Our Lady Who Thinks She Is a Saint" and "Rage Goddess"; *NELLE:* "Heifer" and "Razor Days"; *The Night Heron Barks:* "Brain Fever"; *Ninth Letter:* "Sucker"; *On the Seawall:* "Biopic" and Resting Bitch Face"; *Poetry East:* "Apology"; *River Styx:* "Dolly" and "Our Lady of the Ingrates"; *Sonora Review:* "The Pelegrin in Her Piety"; *Southern Review:* "Our Lady of the Flood"; *Subtropics:* "Royal Ancestry"; *Verse Daily* (reprint): "Our Lady of the Flood" and "Deluge"; *Tin House:* "My Snatch Is Pretty Good"; and *Water~Stone:* "Walking on Water."

Some of these poems appeared in the limited edition chapbook *Our Lady of the Flood* (Diode Editions, 2018), winner of the Diode Chapbook Prize and the Eric Hoffer Award for the chapbook.

I am grateful to the generosity of the Louisiana Board of Regents and Southeastern Louisiana University for the funding and time provided by an ATLAS Grant.

This book has an angel, and her name is Ava Leavell Haymon. Thank you for years of wisdom inspiration, and support.

"Special thanks" seems inadequate, and yet that is what I offer to Bryan Davidson—he knows why.

NOTES

"Denim and Diamonds": A now-defunct glitter/western nightclub, which, when I was a kid, seemed to me the epitome of adulthood and sophistication.

"Feast of the Cajun Navy": If you have a boat and you come to the aid of people stranded by a flood, you are a member of the Cajun Navy. Thank you to the stranger with a boat who delivered me to the ambulance that couldn't reach us.

"The Pelegrin in Her Piety": This is Lingo Sonnet, a form created by Barbara Hamby and which I would describe as a thirteen-line double abecedarian. Hamby did an alphabet of these poems in her book *All-Night Lingo Tango*—I managed two. This one starts with the letter *m,* and the title refers to the pelican in her piety—tearing at her breast to feed her young with drops of her own blood, which is also depicted on the state flag of Louisiana.

"Flood Subject": The floodwaters of my youth, but also Emily Dickinson writing to Thomas Wentworth Higginson on June 9, 1866: "You mention Immortality. That is the flood subject."

"Heifer": At eleven years of age, Saint Maria Goretti was stabbed fourteen times after refusing sexual advances from a grown man. She died soon after, but not before forgiving her attacker.

"Our Lady of the Flood": Inspired by Joe Raedle's photograph. Leigh Babin and her husband T. J. Babin bring items they recovered from their flooded home to shore along with a statue of the Virgin Mary that they found in the flood waters on August 17, 2016, in Sorrento, Louisiana.

"Our Lady of 'No Ragrets'": Patron saint of those who hide regrettable, inappropriate, and misspelled tattoos beneath their clothes

"Messenger": An American Sentence Sonnet, a poetic form originated by Diane Seuss by way of Allen Ginsberg, in which each line of the sonnet is an American sentence of seventeen syllables.

"Deluge": A triple sonnet in the manner of Dorothy Chan.

"The Close Part": *See* "Flood Subject."